Dream, Actually.
A Collection of Poems

by
Isabella Maria Catherine Ramos

Copyright © 2021 Isabella Ramos
Cover Design by David Dzurilla
All rights reserved.
ISBN: 9798484417049

*to all of the people, places, and things
that gave me a why.*

she was never afraid of taking up too much space

her once dainty hands turned into fists that could move mountains

she isn't as small as she used to be

but the universe isn't either

sometimes her words come out in

italics

bold

<u>underline</u>

every punctuation, all at once

don't ever let your words be little

I meticulously crafted each wing
I ardently poured my love into paper
like how you begrudgingly poured
my coffee each sunday
the bitterness of the beans was no match for your
mirroring identity

-paper cranes

I left my happiness in california
manufactured serotonin
comes from purple pills
and plastic palm trees

I wonder if you still pick up your phone
and scroll through old messages
skipping over my name
like the graffiti under the bridge
you pass it every morning on your way to work
but if someone asked you what it said
you couldn't recall a single detail

a bite to the knee,
blood-stained teeth

a soul wounded
before it ever had a chance
to finish growing

some days my feet don't touch the ground

I wander, never to be found

my eyes are heavy, like the moon in the clouds

come home, sister, come home

my eyes *are* a different shade when I wear green

the weather changes them, emotion too

I feel no more shame when I wonder
if you still think of me

and the way my eyes looked when you left

The
Hands
Of
Ultimate
Gratitude
Held
To the
Sky

As
Night
Darkens

Prayer
Reaches
Above
Yet
Everlasting
Renown
Stays

pebbles in my pocket
carry me away
I am a bolder cracking under the pressure
help me be small

you think one hundred million problems are too
much for God to take but He is big enough

if the kingdom of God is big enough
for 7 billion people

it is big enough for you too

is it rain?
or is it just the stale tears
that forgot to fall from last weeks breakdown

you have eyes that tell stories
without you ever having to say a word

I know which direction you will go
with every move you make
but it never leaves me dissatisfied,
even for a second

you make me ponder how predictability can be so
tranquilizing

I can hear the crickets singing their
summer symphony

what have I done to deserve such beautiful music?

do they sing for me, knowing their melody will

ring in my ears until the rising of the sun?

you are never too much

you are vast

beauty beyond compare

it was never about your size

but the complexity of your person

what if I said
I didn't love you
anymore

would you love me then?

I read old books
to transport myself somewhere
I wear old clothes
to be somebody new
I listen to old music
hoping to feel what they felt

all I need to be is here, now

I was finally open for business
two years in the making

no monetary value could repay me
for what you took from me

now I am closed, not for repairs
for good.

we sing of your name like we were born to
when our words fall short, our song never fails
we bring up our hands to share your glory to
all of your children
you reached out to us with nails in your hands

each time we worship, we are creating a brand new
melody, waiting to be debuted,
each prayer creating the next note as we go

unreciprocated love
your heart beats to a different drum,
funny enough it's my favorite song to listen to

my mom never liked the song, anyway

soft, like autumn leaves after a midnight rainfall

warm vanilla sugar, cinnamon and spice
a sunday afternoon scone

you are my perfect cup of coffee

tick
   tick
      tick
my thoughts pierce my brain
like tiny stinging bees
each hurting more than the last
         tick
           tick
It piles up
I break
I explode
I hurt everyone in my radius with the shrapnel
              tick
                tick
                  tick
my mind is a can of soda
that has been shaken one too many times
I know what is inside but do not wish to explore
the mess I will make if it's opened
                        tick
                        Boom.

blessed be my arms
lifting me higher than I thought they ever could

blessed be each hair on my head
that carries me away from the crowd

blessed be the vessel
that is used to house life's most precious gift
not to be despised
blessed be my legs
walking me to horizons only thought of in dreams

blessed be each step I take
strides of elegance led by my feathery feet

it is okay if you do not always see God
in the thousand-year-old cathedral

or in church on a sunday morning

but in the night sky
in the face of your first love
in the innocence of a child

what if I said goodbye for the last time but
you weren't around to hear it?

what if my heart and soul, dripping onto
tear-stained paper never gets the chance to
reach you?

was it my past that scared you away from
a future with me?

you give your opinions out like trading cards

the more you offer, the less valuable they
become to me

sacred plastic bottle

your rattle plays over in my ears

unrecognizable to those

who have never met pain

bliss

like a child's laughter

peace

like the spirit's breath

joy

like your favorite song

a winding road to a familiar place
on the days I wanted it felt like a minute
the days I dreaded felt like a lifetime

a basement
the smell stuck with me for years
the hairspray hairpins hairnets
wigs and costumes filled corners backstage

lockers shared with soulmates
dressing rooms full of secrets
stories that broke my heart off
piece by piece

who knew life could be so damaging until
I met them
my heart soul feelings memories
all in the basement of a building
I never got to see the top of

each and every soul in the
cramped room, plenty of friendly faces
filled mine to make me whole
I'm still learning
but I miss them
I need them
to fill the soul that has emptied since I left

                    -a letter to JCT

moments between the thunder

our innocence was bliss, only for a second

lighting came before we knew it

your hand fidgeted
almost like it was begging me to grab it
I could feel every part of you next to me
not a part of me
I wanted so desperately to have
your hands in my hands
soul in soul

standing in the mirror
admiring the way my ribs stick out of my body
cold fingers on thin skin
I am getting older now
stepping on the scale,
poking at the fat on my body.
ten years old, I am in middle school now
my shirts getting tighter and my cheeks still plump
I was told to hate myself
because loving yourself was arrogant
and I listened.
hiding my weight under shirts two sizes too big
people expect you to be thin
that is the norm, there is no other way

if only I could see myself now.
my size is nothing more than an adjective.

the lights are so bright tonight
I see orbs outside of my window
almost like I live in new york city
instead, it is family's fighting over
the last piece of pizza
people finishing homework from monday

screaming what we have previously learned
there are voices from all directions
but, for some reason, I can only focus
on you

I want to be speeding in my car with you running
red lights after stopping
not touching not looking
I hope that you trust me
pumping my gas
I shivered in the parking lot
I felt so helpless
you didn't seem to care
you lent me your book
there is a great amount of trust in that

I feel bad writing poetry

the same way I feel bad falling asleep in a city that isn't mine

imposter

stranger

unable to be recognized

unable to be found

the subway feels like my hometown

passing unfamiliar faces

in too familiar of places

the third floor smells like friday nights dinner,
waiting at the table for you to come home

the fourth floor is like waking up on a sunday
morning, alarms telling you it's time to go

the stoop is a symphony, longing to be played with
each step you take naming the next note

wandering through the front door creates the music
you were made to be playing

don't be afraid to take the first step

the beginning 9 months of my life
before I came into this earthly world
were spent in darkness
nothing to interrupt my peace
nothing to skew my thoughts

the dim surrounding that I once enjoyed
soon became a darkness that cannot be overcome

sitting in a room
music on, lights off
trying to provide the same satisfaction
allows for a limited perspective of new thoughts
endless possibilities

it is not until I die
that I will receive the darkness that I've longed for
since the beginning of me
and before

one day, the world full of bright lights and
inevitable pitch-black thoughts
will be returned to the eternal peace

I will be but a shadow of black
and that will be enough
no worries, no fears
just darkness
just like the beginning

I never thought my life would reach past the radius
of where I grew up

school busses passing at the same time like
clockwork

every face I passed in the grocery is another hello
waiting to happen

my father feels famous, singing songs everyone
knows

9'oclock on a Saturday, feeling alright

there is something about the word *new*
that feels like a secret message
only we can decipher
one syllable, three letters
holding so much potential
life has changed so many times
life has brought so many unknowns
that we manufactured a word for it
new
words can only be meaningful if you allow it
new
shared stares allow us to know exactly what it
means without ever having to speak
new
washed clean, for the first time over and over again
like the cry of an infant
new
forgiveness does not have an expiration date

your last day was just another Tuesday

7:30- morning announcements

8:00- spanish class

10:45- reading your obituary

your final moments were just another noon passing by

11:30- lunch

12:15- study hall

1:00- lifeless body

my soul aches knowing my normal was your goodbye

I still know your middle name but don't remember
if you are right or left-handed
I know your brother's favorite video game but
not the way your laugh sounds
I remember your favorite feature of yourself but
often forget the things you used to say to me
apple pie will never taste the same as it did before
I met you

every word I say
isn't enough to please you
"I'm sorry" doesn't cut it anymore
empty words
spilling from my lips
I never meant them but
at least they made you happy

depression is the half-eaten pancake you left on
your dresser for 3 weeks
so hard it could break a window
or your heart, if you try hard enough
anxiety is drinking fruit punch wearing a white shirt
driving a semi-truck through new york city
you can do it
but should you?

I think I will go home now
I haven't left my house in a week

I think I'll have to pass
I never even considered it

I am too busy unfortunately
I have nothing in my schedule for the next week

                                                          -anxiety

great is the way you hold me when I am crumbling
faster than the pastry I had for breakfast
great is the feeling I get when I leave your home,
longing for the second I get to return
great is your promise that never fails, never changes
no matter how many days pass
great are the ways you show me you're there
without ever having to say a word
you are waiting to wander the
hallowed halls of my heart

you possess every key to every nook and cranny

not coming in until the invite is made clear

your stories are pyramids

brick by brick, laid meticulously

never forgetting one detail

or your foundation will crumble

my stories are a bouncy castle

cotton candy stained fingers trying to pick up the pieces of my story I left on the ground

clouds of bubbles surrounding what used to be a thought

                      flying

                                    away

light in the window
the beams on my faded face
illuminated

I, the author, and you, the poem on my page

carrying each other through the darkness
we have created

we highlight bullet holes in bright yellow ink

leaving the shell to smear as the words go on

I, the author, romanticize the way I can no longer
read you, the poem, as I smudge what used to be

I miss the sounds you used to make
outside my window every night

the pounding of the oil plant
like music to my ears

I miss the way you greeted me when I came home
worn carpet on tired feet, burnt out lights that were
somehow brighter than the sun

from my window, I swore I saw the universe
or just streetlights too far for me to make out

I miss every imperfection that made you feel
like home.

our friendship, as brief as it is
gives me something good to remember
the joy of reminiscing on jovial times
sharing words only friends would understand
listening to your songs pretending
like I know exactly how
they make you feel

I feel guilt pretending
that I know the way your brain works

but I love you and I mean that
no matter how short or how long
I miss the laughter
from your car in a parking lot or
paint-covered hands, building cardboard trees

being vulnerable is absolutely necessary
breaking every piece of your heart back open
that you thought began to heal

it was never healed
held together by feeble tape,
ready to fall apart at the next occasion

it is not until you your heart is exposed
giving it to the only one who matters most
that you can begin to heal

over and over again it will break
but each moment of vulnerability
only makes the heart grow stronger

as I look at the sunset
I imagine what it would look like
in the reflection of your sunglasses
instead of over the cars passing by
or the trees in my backyard
or the people who don't matter

nothing beats the feeling of a lingering hug
your laugh stays with me all the way home
your smile stays with me forever
if I could count the times I said
I love you
I would never stop talking
someday I hope you begin to hear it

the fourth of july always reminded me of you

the way that your excitement comes from
gunpowder and the glow

lights me up

leaving you is like chasing a mirage that
I will never catch up to

sacrificing my safety just to look into your eyes for

one
    second
        longer

a sprint towards the sunrise
or a swim across the river
will never hold the same significance
after this summer

tears of laughter and cries of joy
at the jokes only a child could tell

do not forget to say hello from the other side

I wonder why our flags fly in different directions

freedom must be in a different spot
in your dictionary

I wish I could say that you are my
home away from home

but you will never be my safety

you will never be my home-cooked meal

you will never be karaoke in my living room

you are here. you are not home.

you speak so quietly
words I don't understand
you hold me so softly
I forget you're even there
you touch me so gently
it's like you're already gone

the way the moon hits the Hudson

is the way your eyes were always beaming

I formed every word I had into a prayer for you

my walls are emptier without you, my prayers no longer pleas but thank you's

the soothing silence of sitting in your soft arms isn't there anymore

your voice as I fall asleep is replaced by the taxis and construction and whistle of the wind outside my window

the bright light in your eyes is now a skyscraper full of people I will never meet, counting the minutes until they get to go home

the thing is, I am home.

I don't need your hand in mine or the crushing cliche of kisses in my car to feel like I am wanted

the smile of a stranger I pass on the street is enough to know I am needed here

I feel bad writing poetry

the same way I feel bad falling asleep in a city that isn't mine

imposter

stranger

unable to be recognized

unable to be found

the subway feels like my hometown

passing unfamiliar faces

in too familiar of places

stranger, oh stranger

you have a gaze that could make a flower bloom

your eyes hold so many stories

but I will never know even one

our eyes met like strangers in a busy museum

sharing waves across a crowded atrium

only to wander and never meet again

and she's my canvas.
my blood, sweat, and tears, smeared on
every blank space.
she absorbs the blue, the red, the yellow, forming a
coherent piece.
or maybe she's the brush that glides across the page,
producing the art.
she is essential to my painting.
she is my piece of art.
without her the page would stay empty
without her there would be nowhere
for the art to go.
nowhere for her beauty to be seen,
or mine

the echo of a leaky pipe is inexplicably harmonious
drip after drip after drip
composing a lullaby as the water trickles down
it puts me to sleep like a cradlesong

I wonder if we knew the first time we met
would be an open door leading to infinite hallways

I wonder if the boat ride was meant to be rocky
because she knew we would both be aboard

I wonder if the next open door will bring us to the
same empty room, pink walls
plastered with our future

the red glow on the pavement lets me know it's time
to go home.
the same signs remind me that maybe I'm just not
trying hard enough
I intentionally divide up my time,
meticulously spending each second
with people who do not matter
forgetting to give seconds to those who taught me to
watch for the red lights in the first place.

there is a point where it becomes too much

when the fighting, bloodshed, pain is no longer
worth my inevitable dissolution

I will leave the door open on my way out, in case
the agony becomes too much for you too

the war is over, it is time to go home

I held onto your love as a child holds
onto a balloon

I was grasping so tight I almost forgot it was in my
hands the whole time

I thought there would never be a pain worse than
letting it slip from my sweaty palms and

float

slipping into another place and time

I hope it never lands in the hands of someone who
will hold on too tight

take advantage of the moments you get to breathe

your days here are numbered, do not miss the moments to make them good

redefine your narrative

you are everything I wish to be when I am older

every hope and dream I hold for myself you have already lived

you look at every star like it is there just for you
because they are

how great is the stardust that lingers in your eyes

the raindrops dance during the storm,
performing their pas de deux.

they arch, arabesque

watch them take their final bow

what a glorious day when the big red X
does not find its way into my vocabulary

three, four, five days pass, and I almost
forget it exists

but the second I fall, it comes right back to my mind
like the popcorn I left in the microwave for
10 seconds too long

burnt out

sometimes when I hear worship music,
I think of you

not because I see you in the presence of God

or because we used to worship side by side

but because I am reminded of all of the things a
man should be when I sing about my God

and you didn't check a single box.

I often consider that my words are not
confined to paper.

the second they are read, they leave their temporary
resting place and fly far beyond my thoughts could
ever comprehend.

treat them kindly, if you will.

Made in the USA
Coppell, TX
30 October 2021